MARGUER

100 THINGS I LOVE ABOUT YOU

IRISH
CANON
PRESS

For Joe, who has changed my life in more ways than I could ever count. Thank you for being you and the love of my life 100 times over!

Kelli,
Cheers to love!
love,
Marguerite

'Relationships [are] Coasters. Remem[ber to throw your hands] up & Laugh [when] you Scream.'

—Marguerite Crespillo

e Like Roller

er to Buckle

Re Than

©2022 by Marguerite Crespillo

Crespillo, Marguerite
100 Things I Love About You: Reignite Your Relationship.

ISBN: 9780996685504 (paperback)

LCSH: Interpersonal relations. | Interpersonal communication. | Communication-- Psychological aspects. | Marriage--Psychological aspects. | Self-realization. | Self-actualization (Psychology) | Resilience (Personality trait) | LCGFT: Self-help publications.

LCC: HM1166 .C74 2022 | DDC: 302.2--dc23

Illustration: © Melinda Maniscalco

First Edition 2022

We hope you enjoy this book from:
Irish Canon Press
2625 Alcatraz Avenue, Suite 105
Berkeley, CA 94705

Introduction

I have told the story of 100 Things I Love About You *hundreds of times to friends and family; at speaking engagements, on podcasts, on the radio, and even to random people that I've met. People who all struggle with a universal problem: the challenges of a relationship, and how to survive the low point when you are ready to throw in the towel and give up.*

Every relationship goes through challenges. Every. Single. One.

When talking to anyone who has been with a partner for long enough, and the relationship survived, they will have stories of their trials and how they worked through them and rebuilt their union.

Relationships, like life, are a roller coaster ride full of highs and lows. We just seem to have a harder time dealing with the lows when it has to do with our home and our emotions.

My husband and I are no different. We went through some of the hardest trials a relationship can face, but, along the way, at the lowest point, I decided that I didn't want to lose my husband and our marriage and so rather than quit, I listened, learned and changed my thinking. I'm sharing my story with you and the power of writing 100 Things, hopeful that this book causes you to pause and consider what would be lost, and then in some small but meaningful way, helps you to reignite your love and relocate the soul of your relationship.

'You know You're in Love when You Can't Fall 👁 Asleep Because Reality is Finally Better than Your dreams'

-Dr. Seuss

1

The Moment

Everyone has their story. The story of how they met. The first time they felt the butterflies in their stomach. The moment they decided this might turn out to be more than just friendship or a passing acquaintance. Ask any couple how they met, and their eyes light up. They get that funny smirk on their face as they go back and remember the moment.

Here's our story...

I met Joe in April of 1986. I was an inexperienced woman, even for twenty-two years old. I had just left a relationship. I'd thrown everything in my car and was in a new city and ready for an adventure.

My mom had been telling me since the day I graduated from high school that I needed to venture out of our small town and explore the world. I was finally ready, so I reached out to my favorite uncle, who lived seventy miles south of us in Sacramento. I thought I would stay with him until I found work and had a plan.

My uncle knew a gal and, understanding that I needed friends, he introduced us. Nancy was a hairstylist who had converted the garage of her house into a salon. Coming from a small town, I was not only naive, I had never done much with my hair, and I really didn't even know how to wear makeup. Nancy gave me a complete style makeover.

The first thing she did was color and perm my hair. (And because it was the 80's, she gave me some really big hair!) As I was sitting in the chair admiring my new puffy locks and make-over, in walked a friend of hers.

He had jet black hair, untied high-top tennis shoes with tight fitting blue jeans and an untucked dress shirt. He shuffled in with his head hung low followed by a date—who clearly was not happy.

Nancy said: "Hey Joey, meet my friend Marguerite."

He continued walking and when he reached the door into her house he turned and with a nod of his head said: "Hey, what was your name again?"

"Marguerite," I replied.

With a half grin, he turned and walked into the house.

Although his good looks had caught my attention, he was with a date, so I didn't think much of it.

A couple of weeks later, Nancy and I decided to go out dancing. We were opposite one another at a stand-up bar. And, of course, in walked Joe. This time his head was held high, he was wearing a three-piece suit, laughing, joking, and with a different date.

He sat down next to Nancy, his date sat next to me.

He was really cocky, an obvious player. Every time his

date would look the other way, he would wink at me. I was new in town and I must admit, it was a big ego boost. My confidence was struggling due to my recent breakup, along with the fact that I had no idea what I was going to do with my life.

But I also knew that, as handsome as this guy was, he was bad news.

We finished our drinks and I motioned to Nancy that we should go. We got up, excused ourselves and went next door to another dance club. About 45 minutes later, in walked Joe again. This time, without the date! He had taken her home and had come back for me.

Enjoying his attention, I remember thinking... well, maybe we can just have some fun dancing, but nothing more! We danced once, twice... I was heading right into trouble... and I liked it. But a cooler head prevailed and I knew that I better not go down that road. Leaving the dance floor, I quickly pulled Nancy aside to say goodbye and left before Joe knew I'd gone.

The next day, Nancy handed me Joe's business card and said that he was disappointed that I had left without saying goodbye. He'd asked her to ask me to contact him. I laughingly threw that card in the garbage and thought "Not happening!"

Never say never.

A few days later I learned that I had to immediately move out of my storage unit back in my hometown. This meant I had to find a truck, but because of my age, I couldn't rent one. The only person I knew who might be able to help was Nancy. And, of course, the only person she knew with a truck was Joe.

A million thoughts went through my head, but the overwhelming one was that if I called Joe, he would think this was an excuse, and he would have the upper hand. That didn't seem like a good idea. Call it fate, destiny, poor-decision-making when it came to men, or being 22, I felt I had no choice but to call and ask to borrow his truck.

I swallowed my pride and reluctantly picked up what felt like a two-ton telephone. He quickly answered and said I could use his truck on one condition: that I go out to dinner with him! I felt my face get red and thought, ok, I'll just use his truck and brush him off.

After moving the last of my possessions from the warehouse, I dropped off his truck.

"What are you doing tonight?" he asked.

"I have plans with Nancy."

"Great! What time should I come over?"

Laughing and pretending to ignore his comment, I thanked him for the truck, got in my car and took off. That evening I was sitting comfortably on the couch at Nancy's watching a movie when Joe came blasting through the door: "Thanks for waiting for me!"

He poured himself a drink and plopped down on the couch next to me. Little by little, he kept moving closer. I tried to ignore whatever was happening between us, but it became overwhelming as he brushed his hand against my leg.

Then he looked closely at me with his big brown eyes, and I felt my life was about to get a lot more exciting. He leaned in and whispered in my ear, "Wanna go for a drive?"

Your first assignment is to REMEMBER. Sit and close your eyes. No matter how you are feeling about your partner at this exact time, think back to when you first met and what it felt like. What time of year was it? Where were you? What was your first impression? Write about YOUR MOMENT.

2

Expectations

Everyone has them. Especially expectations about how a relationship should be. We get them from watching our own parents, our grandparents, our neighbors (through their open curtains), and from anyone who raised or influenced us. We get them, good or bad, from romantic comedies and social media posts. We develop this idea in our head about how a relationship is supposed to be. We imagine the perfect relationship. The romantic who sweeps us off our feet. The perfect partner who is always dressed well and cooks amazing food.

Ok, maybe that is a little far fetched... but is it? The big problem with these expectations is they are usually a story that you have created in your mind that no one else knows about but you.

Let me explain... when you were young, you probably had a secret crush. Maybe it was on the boy in grade school with the crooked smile or the girl in your freshman year class with the long flowing hair and sparkling eyes. You dreamt about them. You wrote notes to them that you never delivered. You imagined what it would be like to hold their hand or kiss them. You spent hours thinking about what fun you would have together.

And then... you actually got to talk to them, spend time with them, and you quickly realized they were not at all like you expected them to be. Maybe you see the couple on social media who constantly post about their romantic adventures and the love notes they write to one another. It seems like they have the perfect life. Love stories at the movies may show difficult times in the middle of the movie, but the ending almost always includes dramatic, romantic, full-spring leaps back into one another's loving arms.

What you don't see are the battles and arguments of real life, nor the nasty, messy stuff that happens behind the scenes, that no one posts on social media.

All these scenarios cause you to look at your own relationship and expect things to be like what you see being portrayed all around you. It creates a set of expectations that are usually not conveyed to your partner, but kept instead in the secret vault of your mind.

Of course, it becomes a bit of a setup of sorts. You expect your partner to behave a certain way, but they have no idea what your expectations are. It really is unfair and unrealistic to keep those expectations a secret.

Yet it happens all the time and is a huge challenge in relationships.

What did you think your relationship was going to be like?
Have your expectations been met and have they changed over
time? Have you shared them and if you haven't, why not?

'The emoti
bReak Your
SOMetimes
that heals

N Ahat CaN

eaRt ♥ is

he VERy ONe

- Nicolas Sparks

3

What Was I Thinking?

When I fell in love with Joe, he had three children, a girl and two boys, and was going through a divorce. Though not yet legally married, overnight, I became a mom. Being twenty-two-years old and from a dysfunctional background, it felt glamorous to have an instant family. I'd always wanted a big, stable clan, and this seemed like a shortcut to one.

I was naive, thinking it would be easy. I thought I could move right into this ready-made family and skip the part of building a foundation based on hard work and sacrifice.

I soon came to learn that it's just as difficult being a stepparent as a biological parent. Being a young stepmother meant that there was another person, the kids' mom, involved in almost each and every decision we made. She was there to override any decisions I made as a stepparent and, in most situations, rightfully so.

Joe and his ex were *the parents*. I was just their father's girlfriend.

Now to be clear, we are extremely lucky that we have a great relationship with my husband's ex. But this scenario came with a ton of work, numerous near-nervous breakdowns, and other challenges, both large and small.

Thankfully, everything always came down to what was best for the children. Whatever the reasons and whatever the cost, if there are children involved you will need to have a relationship with all the parents for as long as you live. You might as well find a way to make it positive and peaceful for everyone.

It is my belief that the difficulties with many blended families are that people tend to remember the worst parts of their prior relationships, rather than the best. Joe and his ex-wife are terrific people, they simply weren't a good married couple. Once we sat down, moved our egos out of the way, and communicated, we quickly realized that all our hearts were in the right places. We needed to get past hurt feelings, see our true natures, and realize we were all in this for life. The one common thread we would always have was the children. We embraced that idea, and life became much easier.

My bottom line was that I fell in love with Joe. Not only was Joe handsome and funny, but he is a great father and I wanted to be around that.

My mother had been married four times and I didn't have a stable father figure. It was one of the things I loved most about him and I needed to help him continue to be
that great dad.

What are one or two key qualities or experiences that your partner brought into the relationship that made you fall in love with them? Do you know how that fits into your wishes and dreams?

4

Falling Apart

Though in love, Joe and I had been together less than two rocky years, navigating dating, his divorce, bonus kids, and, suddenly, a surprise pregnancy.

Frankly, before we found out I was expecting, we were not even sure we were going to stay together. Our news brought about in-depth conversations regarding where we were in our relationship and what our future might look like. We decided that regardless of whether we ultimately stayed together long term or not, we would focus on being great parents to our new child.

Our beautiful son Jordon either brought us closer together or it helped to mask our differences, it's hard to say which. Joe, who is nothing if not a wonderful father, and I began growing stronger and more stable together.

Then things suddenly turned tragic when we were hit with life-changing news.

When Jordon was four, he got very sick with chicken pox and strep throat, and then suddenly went into a coma. We rushed him to the hospital, where panicked doctors tried to figure out what was going on. After several hours, he was diagnosed with Addison's disease. They gave him cortisol, which brought him out of the coma.

Over the next weeks and months, there were dozens of doctors' appointments, along with hours of research, all trying to determine what was happening in our little boy's body, and what it meant for his future. We quickly became experts about the disease. We learned that Addison's is when the adrenal glands don't produce enough of the hormone cortisol (and sometimes aldosterone). When the body is under stress (fighting an infection), this cortisol deficiency can result in a life-threatening "Addisonian crisis" characterized by extremely low blood pressure. It is a potentially lethal condition, which is more likely to be deadly the younger the patient is when diagnosed.

Looking back at my family history, my father had passed away when I was ten years old. My parents were already divorced, and not only did we hardly ever see him, I was given almost no information about how he died. I was told later that he had Addison's disease, which didn't mean much to me until Jordon's diagnosis. Yet when Jordon was diagnosed, we were told it was not genetic.

We were confused, but that was secondary. Not only was our son extremely sick, we intuitively realized it was only the beginning.

Eventually, we were referred to an institute in
Baltimore, Maryland, which was conducting research on

Adrenoleukodystrophy, made famous by the film, *Lorenzo's Oil*. We began to fly there every six months for testing and further research with Jordon.

But nothing helped.

Four years later, when Jordon turned eight, we were informed that the disease was progressing, and that he would need a bone marrow transplant.

By this time, we had two more boys: Jacobo, two years old, and Jon, who was one. We had tested our entire family and found that while Jacobo was not a carrier, Jon was a carrier and so was I. There was so much guilt that went along with this time in our lives. I felt like it was my fault. How could I deal with not only one child with this disease but two?

Joe and I cried for days. Finally, pulling ourselves together, we knew we had to move forward. The good news: Jacobo was a perfect bone marrow donor match to Jordon.

So, we did what we had to do. We packed up our family and moved to Minnesota for six months while Jordon underwent his transplant. We rented a small apartment near the hospital and rotated between staying with Jordon and taking care of Jacobo and Jon. We were very blessed in that our nanny, Rosalie, one of the kindest people I've ever known, came with us to help with the children.

So, how do you keep your relationship intact when you are dealing with a seriously ill child?

We didn't.

The fact is, that we went through the motions and barely spoke. We were angry at the world and that meant we were angry with one another. We did what needed to be done and, frankly, most of the time it was too difficult to discuss.

Somehow, the earth kept spinning.

I learned quickly that just because you have a sick child doesn't mean anything else comes to a stop. For starters, Joe was downsized from his job as a bank vice president due to a rash of bank mergers. And we dealt with Jordon's illness differently. Joe was almost inconsolably depressed over the declining health of our formerly fun-loving son, and the derailment of his career.

I just worked. In fact, it was while working that I got some relief from life. More and more we found ourselves struggling down separate paths of despair that rarely crossed. For long periods of time we rarely made eye contact. Strangely, I don't remember all that much about that time. Dealing with a terminally ill child, two young children, working full time and struggling with our marriage and with life was too overwhelming.

One evening I was on my way home from work, manic and desperate to escape the pain, I remember actually speeding in the hope that the police would take me to jail so that I could get away from my life and go to sleep.

But I couldn't even summon a traffic ticket. Not only did I not get pulled over, but when I got home, I walked through the door and all three of my children were crying, "Mommy! Mommy! Mommy!" Joe was just standing behind them looking like a lost little boy.

I remember thinking to myself that he was just one more challenge for me to endure. One more responsibility. I was barely able to breathe, much less take care of all the
responsibilities that were stacking up in our lives.

Worst of all, our Jordon didn't get any better. He continued his steady decline, going from a vibrant, lively eight-year old, to eventually losing his vision, his hearing, and, later, his mental abilities.

Looking back, it all still seems like one long horrible nightmare. Our lovely Jordon died at the age of 10 on a summer day in June of 1999.

I was mad at the world and I hated my place in life. I hated the father I never knew. I hated my mother. I hated Joe. I hated the doctors. The yard. The sky. The voice on the phone. And I wanted to hurt someone or something. I just wanted everything to be different than how it was.

Whenever I looked at Joe, I knew one thing: working on my marriage to him wasn't my priority.

SoMetiMes
to Fall APARt
Much they N
Back togethe

People have
to Realize how
D to Fall

— Anonymous

5

Which Way Do I Go?

Most relationships have a turning point. Some have multiple turning points. Turning points that define which way everything can or will go. I see it more like a four-way stop sign.

The kind of four-way intersection with a stop sign in every direction and someone sitting at each stop, waiting for someone else to make a decision and go first. You all stare at one another. The tension builds. Then you start getting anxious and even irritated. Finally, someone takes the plunge and starts to go, but then the others also start to go, and then everyone stops.

Eventually, you all figure it out or you'd spend half your life at four-way-stop intersections.

When a relationship gets to that corner, it seems you are both waiting for someone to make a decision. That awkward moment: Should I go? Should I stay? Should I let them go first? Wait, they really should go first. But wait a minute, it's my turn. No, it's their turn.

The bottom line is, if you decide to leave, (and this is something I see more often than not) you end up leaving, finding a bright, shiny new person, but all the same problems arise because you never worked out the deeper issues within yourself before taking the leap (and, if you had worked them out, you might not have left to begin with).

If your relationship is in turmoil, there's always hope. But, at some point, a decision must be made, and I encourage you to be the one to make it. Be the first to say, "I am sorry." Be the one who says, "I love you."

Has there been a specific incident or incidents in your relationship that brings you to a turning point?

6

Attorney or Counselor?

I woke up one morning and I knew I was at the end of my relationship. I'd had enough and was ready to leave. I rolled over and looked at Joe who was peacefully sleeping. He had no idea what was about to hit him. Pushing him awake, I stated, "Today is the day."

"What?" he mumbled, shaking sleep from his mind.

"Today is the day we either go to an attorney or a counselor, but we will schedule an appointment with one or the other by the end of the day... and the decision is entirely up to you."

He shook his head a couple times and said, "What?"

"You heard me!" I slammed out of the room.

A few hours later, I got a message that we had an appointment with a counselor for the next day.

And, suddenly, the smallest glimmer of hope flickered in my heart.

Appointment One

I sat in front of the counselor with my arms crossed and a scowl on my face. It was easy to figure out that I didn't want to be there. The counselor looked back and forth between us and asked "Why are you here?"

"Because she made me..." Joe started in his typical joking tone.

That joke did not go over well. I angrily stood to walk out when he grabbed my arm and said, "Don't go."

Appointment Two

We talked about our family backgrounds. We came from very different worlds. Joe was from an old-world Spanish family. His parents had been married for over fifty years. He was the baby of eight children and an unexpected gift late in life for his forty-five and fifty-five-year-old parents. They loved him and doted on him. He was the center of everyone's attention and he liked it that way.

I was the complete opposite. My mother was strong, independent and had been married four times. None of the marriages lasted long. I had no strong, positive male role models. Frankly, I had seen my mother survive without a husband. I didn't give a husband or father figure all that much value.

My father died when I was ten and I'd only seen him a few times. So, the only relationships I really ever saw (and could model) were dysfunctional ones that didn't last long. I had learned well that it is easier to move on than stick around through the tough stuff.

Appointment Three

This one was when we were asked to come separately. I entered the room, sat down and the counselor asked, "So are you done or is there a glimmer of hope we can work this out?"

"I suppose there is a glimmer." I said, tears welling up in my eyes.

He said, "Well, then I have some homework for you and it may be easy, or it may be hard. That part will be up to you. I want you to make a list of all the things you love about Joe."

"Oh, I already did the pro's and con's and it didn't go well." I laughed.

"No cons," he said. "I think you have that part down."

I admit that stung a little bit.

"I want you to focus on the pro's," he said. "Make a list of the things you love about him. In fact, make a list of 100 Things."

"100 Things?!?! Are you crazy? I am not sure I can think of one right now!"

"Take some time," he said.

I left his office. Getting in my car, I laughed through my tears. 100 Things I Love About Joe? There was no way I could do that. For a number of days, I didn't give the list any thought. Then I woke up one morning to a cup of tea left by Joe at my bedside and thought, "Well, there's one."

1. **Makes me tea every morning.**
   Later, returning from the gym after working out, Joe strode into the bedroom, still looking great.

2. Stays in shape.

At dinner I noticed our kids giggling at one of his dad jokes.

3. Makes our children laugh.

It wasn't easy, and the truth is that I never made it to 100. I only made it to forty-five.

But, the great part is, that with each thing I wrote down, my heart started to soften. My focus shifted from all the things that hurt or made me angry, to all the things that made me fall madly in love with Joe in the beginning. The list allowed me to see and feel the love all over again. I will also tell you that, honestly, Joe didn't really change much of anything. Nope, I did the changing. In fact, I changed my focus.

It is interesting to me how easy it is to focus on all the bad stuff. How quickly we can get obsessed with what is wrong and let it consume our daily thoughts and impact our mood. Yet in the beginning, we don't seem to notice any of those things at all.

And if you're looking for something bigger and deeper than that, or a magic pill, you might be disappointed. But I'd still like for you to give this a shot. I did.

In fact, start now.

Wherever you are in your relationship, whatever mood you are in at this moment, write down ten things you love about your partner...

4. Reminds Me to take My Vitamins.

5. Is A great Dad!

1 I Love...

_____

_____

2 I Love...

_____

_____

3 I Love...

_____

_____

4 I Love...

_____

_____

5 I Love...

_____

_____

6 I Love...

_____

_____

7 I Love...

_____

_____

8 I Love...

9 I Love...

10 I Love...

'The Way I See it, if You Want the 🌈 RaiNBow You Gotta put up With the Rain.' -Dolly Parton

7

Differences

Since the toilet paper spool was invented, there has been the never-ending discussion as to which way it should dispense. It is a pretty good analogy for how relationships evolve, as well.

When you first fall in love, everything your partner does is cute, makes you smile, and you cannot wait to see them, touch them, and spend time with them. They are your entire world and you become consumed with everything they do. You think about them non-stop and can't wait another minute to be with them again.

Then it's your eighth month anniversary (yes, you still celebrate every month!). You are in their home and you see the toilet paper is turned the wrong way (whichever way that is) and you think, "Oh how cute is that? They turn their toilet paper the wrong way." And you chuckle.

But when you have been together a year or so, you

try to politely explain why they should hang the spool your way. You explain in detail why it makes sense to you and all the reasons why they should do things your way. And you both smile and nod at each other with that vague "whatever" look in your eyes.

By year three, it's: "Could you just put the damn toilet paper roll on like I asked you to? It is the only thing I care about, so why can't you just do it my way?"

Now, I make light of this fact for a reason: It is all the little things that happen on a daily basis that seem to get all bunched up in a big ball inside us until someone explodes.

Then year five, it's: "I'll just do it myself!"

Because it's not worth the hassle or the argument, you begin to pick your battles.

In the beginning, we like little differences. Later, they irritate us and cause us untold duress. Maybe it's that one thing that never gets put away in the same place. It's how they drive, or that they tell the same stories over and over.

Joe, who is now a stand-up comedian, says it like this: "In the beginning, she thought everything I said was funny. Now, she says, 'So is everything a damn joke to you?!?'"

Does this sound familiar?

The truth is many of the things that we fell in love with at the beginning eventually become the things that seem to drive us batty later on.

It's you accepting that toilet paper works exactly the same whether it rolls out over the top or the... bottom.

Can you also make a vow to love those things and never complain about them, ever again?

Embrace your differences. What do you love about your partner that is different from you?

11 I Love...

12 I Love...

13 I Love...

14 I Love...

15 I Love...

16 I Love...

17 I Love...

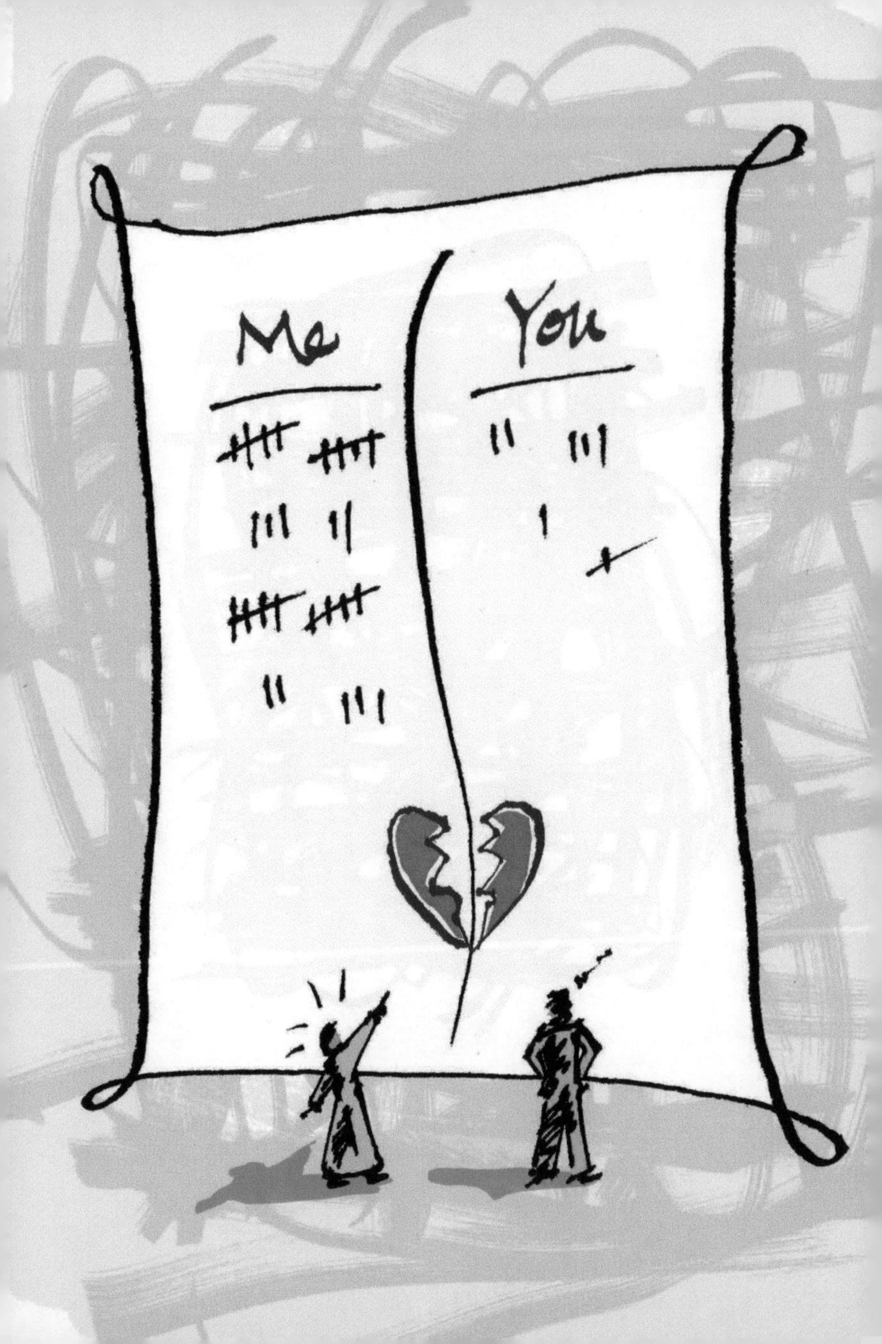
Me
You

8

Change Your Perspective

You might wonder, "Did Joe make a 100 Things I Love list also?" No, he didn't. The list was my homework, not his. We each have different work in life and changing my perspective was my homework.

This is an important point because it may be that both people in the relationship make a 100 Things I Love list, or it may be just one of you. The list is not a competition and it's not about the number. It's about changing your focus or perspective. It's about moving from negative to positive.

When I was given the assignment, I was so angry, frustrated, and ready to walk away from our marriage. I wasn't sure I could come up with even one thing that I loved about Joe. But, after several days of thinking about it, and finally starting to write things down, my focus started to shift from that of anger and frustration to love

47

and gratitude.

What are you focused on?

It can be easy to find the faults in others. Ironically, we rarely see those same faults in ourselves, and, if we do, we place more weight on our partner's faults than our own. As Wayne Dyer wrote: "If you change the way you look at things, the things you look at change." As soon as I decided to step back, look at my own actions, and remind myself what I loved about Joe, it became easier to stop blaming him, and start talking with him instead—which I had not been doing much of at that time.

It's also easy to keep score in a relationship. "I took out the garbage last week, so it's your turn this week." That's not healthy. Depending on what stage of the relationship you're in, the focus and scoring changes.

Early in a relationship we want to do everything possible to impress and we go over the top to show them our best sides. This doesn't seem to bother us in the least. In fact, we love doing it. We wear our best clothes. We call first and say sweet things. We leave love notes. We buy gifts. We do extra things around the house.

Somewhere along the line, however, these acts start to wane. Then we start to keep score. Not only do we stop doing all the wonderful things, but we start tracking what our partner isn't doing, to determine what, if anything, we are going to do.

I have been guilty on multiple occasions of having a meltdown moment where I list out "Everything I am doing," and, for good measure, add in "Everything that Joe is NOT doing" which never ends well (as you can imagine).

'A Relationship is like a house. When a lightbulb burns out you do not go and buy a new house. You fix the lightbulb.'

— Anonymous

The difference between relationships that survive, and ones that don't, is how quickly we realize what is happening and do something to fix it.

There are two things that I realized about these score-keeping marathons, or let's call them "conversations." First, I had not been expressing my expectations effectively. And, second, that Joe did a hell of a lot more than I realized, it's just that I wasn't seeing it.

What things do you love that your partner does for you, your family, or friends that you may not be appreciating?

18 I Love...

19 I Love...

20 I Love...

21 I Love...

22 I Love...

9

What's Most Important?

Our boys Jake and Jon were about seven and eight years old. Jacobo loved animals and had a hamster that he was crazy about. One day the hamster got loose and disappeared. He was heartbroken.

Fast forward a few days later, Joe and I were arguing about something. Frankly, I don't even remember what it was about, but it had escalated to the point that I told him to "get your stuff and get out!" Achieving critical dramatic mass, I grabbed the boys and locked us in the bedroom.

I could hear Joe shuffling around out in the hallway and, a few minutes later, he knocked on the door and said "Jacobo, I found your hamster."

Jacobo jumped up, ran and opened the door to find Joe holding his hamster. He turned around and said: "See, mom, dad is not such a bad guy."

My heart melted. I had been so consumed with being right about whatever we were arguing about that I could not see past the moment and my anger and frustration. Sometimes our ego takes control and being right gets in the way of being in love.

I had to choose what is most important: the relationship or being right. I've had to make this decision repeatedly and practice it. It has been challenging for me, more challenging than a difficult dance move, and more than learning to breathe correctly when swimming.

Ask yourself right now: what's more important, my relationship, or being right?

What about your partner melts your heart?

23 I Love...

24 I Love...

25 I Love...

26 I Love...

What are the most important things about your relationship?

27 I Love...

28 I Love...

29 I Love...

30 I Love...

31 I Love...

10

Do Your Eyes Light Up?

When my kids were little, I met an older woman who was sitting on a bench in the park where they were playing. I was being a little bit impatient with my three-year-old son and she noticed.

She said, "Do you mind if I give you a bit of advice?" I rolled my eyes to myself, but I said, "Sure." She said, "All a child wants is when they run up to you on the playground or they walk into the room to talk to you, is to see your eyes light up."

I looked at her, paused for a moment, and said, "Thank you."

I started to make every effort I could to put her advice into action, and to make certain that my children saw my eyes light up (when I saw them) as much as was humanly possible.

I even experimented that night when Joe came home

from work. I stopped what I was doing and felt the happiness that he was now with our family. I made sure it showed in my eyes. It felt miraculous really, as it not only changed how I felt about him, but his pleasant reaction inspired me to do it more!

Isn't this something everyone wants? We do it when we have not seen someone we love and care about for a long time. What if we made a conscious effort to give our love our full attention and do it all the time? Think of your partner right now and use your expression to show them how much you love them and how happy you are to see them.

What lights you up?

32 I Love...

33 I Love...

34 I Love...

35 I Love...

What secrets do you share that light you up?

36 I Love...

37 I Love...

38 I Love...

39 I Love...

40 I Love...

'Sexiness Wea
while & Bea
to be Married
Makes You Laa
Ah Now that's A

thin afteR A
ty fadeS, But
o A MaN WHO
♥ EveRy DAy,
al treat. —JoaNNe
WooDwaRd

What pop culture, music, festivals, or celebrations do you share a love of?

41 I Love...

42 I Love...

43 I Love...

44 I Love...

45 I Love...

When it comes to your partner, what are their best qualities?

46 I Love...

47 I Love...

48 I Love...

49 I Love...

50 I Love...

11

The Hardest Words

Growing up, I loved to lay on the couch and watch *Happy Days*. The star, Fonzie, was the coolest dude, donning a leather jacket and a tight T-shirt—just the kind of man I liked! He was a smart-ass and everyone on the show loved him, but when he made a mistake, he didn't know how to apologize, and would just stammer instead.

A "dramatic" moment in the show would occur (usually, Richie Cunningham wouldn't know how to kiss a girl), someone on the show would be upset, and Fonzie would try to say the words, "I'm sorry," but he could never get the words to come out right.

The reason I remember this so well is that, when it came to apologizing, I was once a lot like Fonzie. (My mother taught me never to apologize, and if someone else did, she would usually say "you don't really mean it.")

There have been many times in my life when it seemed so painful to say the simple words: "I'm sorry."

Then I met Joe. He apologized for every mistake, but I truly felt like they were just words. He couldn't possibly mean he was really sorry. One day we were fighting about him apologizing to me for something, and me not believing he meant it, when he said: "Which time don't you think I meant it?" and "How can I possibly say 'I'm sorry' in a way that you will believe me? Because no matter when or how I say it, you don't believe me."

That's when I finally heard him.

Because I was so insecure, I couldn't believe that he was sincere and cared about how I felt, so I didn't believe him. Honestly? He was right. He could never say it in a way so that I truly believed him. But what if I just started believing him? How different would that make things?

It was time to try. I began saying, "I'm sorry" too. I would stutter and stop and choke, but eventually I got better at it... I'm still a work in progress.

After all, if you're truly sorry, it doesn't do either of you any good unless you learn to say it, out loud.

What surprising or unexpected things have you come to love about your partner?

51 I Love...

52 I Love...

53 I Love...

54 I Love...

55 I Love...

56 I Love...

57 I Love...

58 I Love...

12

It's Not Always Personal

There are a lot of different opinions about why you marry the person you do. Some say, "You marry the person who heals your wounds from childhood." Others believe that you end up with someone either just like you or the complete opposite of you. No matter what you think, however, the two of you are different people and you have unique backgrounds, thoughts, and ways that you do things.

I remember going to a conference where they had me do a DISC profile test, or a personality test.

I was not surprised at all by my results, but one thing did surprise me: there was a section which described how you see yourself, followed by another section that explained how others see you. I remember thinking they can't possibly be right to see me that way, but when I showed it to my husband he just laughed and said, "That's dead on!"

67

So, I asked Joe to take the test, and thinking that I knew my husband better than anyone, I was sure I knew what the results would be. And yet... his results came back the complete opposite of what I had expected!

Why did this matter? Because it helped me to understand that many of our actions are the result of our personality type and style. It is our projecting onto others, and not necessarily their behavior (they're not trying to mess with anyone else's happiness) that is the key.

In the DISC profile test, I am a HIGH D personality, and Joe is a HIGH I. We have very different styles and ways we do things—neither one is right or wrong, just different.

The differences between us are, firstly, the exact things we both fell in love with, and, secondly, precisely what keeps us in balance. The great thing is, that when we know what those differences are, we can embrace and support our partner instead of criticizing and trying to change them.

Before taking the personality test, and then reading one of my all time favorite books, *The Four Agreements* by Don Miguel Ruiz, I used to take so many things personally. I wish I had read this book earlier in my marriage, because after this small tweak in perception I was better able to understand that everything is not personal and that everything is not about me.

I would quickly lose count if I tried to remember all the arguments Joe and I have ever had simply because one of us was having a bad day, or because something went wrong on the way home, or at work, or one of us walked through the door with a grumpy look on our face. Too often, it went pretty much like this:

"How was your day?"

"Fine."

"What's wrong?"

"Nothing, just had a rough day."

"Well, what happened?"

"Can we talk about it later?"

"No, let's talk about it now. What did I do wrong?"

"Nothing. It's not about you."

"Well clearly you are mad at me about something."

Mistakes:

1. Taking everything personally
2. Bringing up the past
3. And again...taking everything personally.

So now that we know you have two different personalities, what similarities and common interests do you love sharing?

59 I Love...

60 I Love...

61 I Love...

62 I Love...

63 I Love...

13

Fake It Until You Make It

You may have used this line to feign competence when selling yourself or a product. Fake it until you make it can not only help you land your dream job, it can save your dream relationship.

So, what do I mean when I say this?

Here's the deal: The butterflies you may have had when you met are a trick. A trick to get you in the door, so to speak, but they won't keep you there. In reality, it is a feeling that ebbs and flows depending on the thoughts in your head and the ebb and flow of your day-to-day life. The best part...you can control those thoughts.

Most people give the ebbs and flows a label. When they feel butterflies, they connect that feeling to being IN love as opposed to just loving them. We have heard someone say, "I love him, but I am not IN love with him."

In my opinion, what they are referring to are those

dang butterflies.

There have been many times in our relationship where both of us, at different times, either "loved" or were "in love" with the other. [What is interesting to me is when you are in the mode of "just" loving the other person and not "in love," you feel as if you are missing out on something you deserve or that you have lost.]

Do you really think you will find someone who makes you feel those butterflies nonstop? Is it even humanly possible to stay in that high place all the time? We might want to believe it's possible, but that is NOT the real world. That's because very few of us are unconditional with our love.

I'm not trying to be harsh or tell you not to dream. I am NOT saying settle for less than you deserve. What I do know is that in all our years together there have been countless times when we felt one way or the other. Neither one is wrong, but the one thing I do know is that the "in love" extreme when you feel the butterflies really helps you appreciate those times you don't.

So, when you feel butterflies, they are a reminder to take a deep breath and appreciate all the awesomeness in your relationship that will get pushed to the back burner when life gets hard and those butterflies lose their wings.

Go back and remember the last time you felt those butterflies (it doesn't matter how long ago it was). Visualize everything about it. Where you were, what you were wearing, the lighting in the room, even the smells. Remember when you looked at that person and embrace the "something" that made you have those butterflies.

Can you remember?

Now close your eyes for a moment and really zero in on that feeling.

When you open your eyes, go find your partner with that twinkle in your eye and give him or her a great big hug and thank them for being in your life.

All too often, we think it is the BIG things that get in the way of our love, but just as often, it's not letting the small things back in. Or just as big a problem is that we forget that we don't have anything better or more important to do right this minute than to tell our partner we love them.

Now let your mind wander back. Think about some of the best, most memorable moments you've ever experienced with your partner, and add those to your list.

64 I Love...

65 I Love...

66 I Love...

67 I Love...

68 I Love...

Now imagine your brightest moments together and add them.

69 I Love...

70 I Love...

71 I Love...

72 I Love...

73 I Love...

14

Rules

Almost everything has rules. Rules of the games, rules where you work, rules on the highway, and rules of the relationship. While most of the rules we follow are written, the rules of relationships are often unspoken.

This leads to an ongoing battle over their interpretation.

One night, friends were sharing their long list of relationship rules over dinner with Joe and me. We looked at one another and laughed, realizing that we had plenty of our own rules. The issue is, that we had never bothered to agree on them!

We decided then and there to be sure that we were in agreement, and that meant it was time to sit down and discuss them (or perhaps we needed to fight about the rules a bit too!).

In the end, we decided there were only two primary rules, and they were never to be broken. Basically, the rules were simply to improve our life together and make our relationship work better.

The Primary Rules:

One: Never call each other bad names. Calling each other derogatory or hurtful names is not only disrespectful, it cuts deeply and will not be forgotten. Bad names should never be used sarcastically, in a joke, or in a seemingly affectionate way. That is violating the rule and it's passive aggressive.

Two: Never talk about divorce. Not in your mind and not out loud. If you commit to the fact that divorce is not an option, you will work harder on your relationship. You will get creative and look for ways to make it better. If divorce is an option, imagination and intention will inflate that negative outlook and it will become your reality. It will become the inevitable option.

Admittedly, we have accidentally broken our rules a few times, but we quickly see our mistake and work to fix the damage. Over time, we've learned to be much more thoughtful and careful.

Now? the primary rules are an essential part of our marriage. As partners we uphold standards, influence each other and work to be our best selves together...

Are there unspoken rules that you have established in your relationship? As a side assignment, schedule some time with your partner to agree upon your rules *together*. These are the most important rules of your relationship, so only a few are needed. Agree on a final list together, and then write them and keep them.

What things that have nothing to do with you, do you love about your partner?

74 I Love...

75 I Love...

76 I Love...

77 I Love...

78 I Love...

79 I Love...

80 I Love...

81 I Love...

15

Keep It Fun

If you have been together for more than a few years, you may have had a conversation around your anniversary (assuming one of you remembers you have an anniversary!) that went a bit like this:

"What do you want to do for our anniversary?"

"I don't know, what do you want to do?"

"I don't know. Want to go out to dinner?"

"Sure! Where do you want to go?"

"I don't care, where do you want to go?"

This can go on for a while until one of you either gets frustrated or concedes and throws out a random place to eat. (This gets old!) We are treating an opportunity to keep our relationship a priority (and our love flourishing) as some random task we just must endure.

It is also common that one partner is more sentimental, or just better with dates and details, than the other. If you happen to be the partner that doesn't keep track of your anniversary, then you may have unwittingly let your partner down, hurt their feelings, or angered them. If you are the one who remembers the dates and occasions, you may feel resentful that you are the one who always makes plans.

It took us eight years to figure out that we needed to do things differently, so we created a set of Secondary Rules for our anniversary.

Each year we alternate whose responsibility it is to not only make a plan, but to also be in charge of executing it! The best part about this: it has become a little bit of a competition. (In this instance, competition is fun and useful.)

We also have a subset of rules within The Anniversary Rule:

One: If it is your year to make plans, they must be focused on the happiness of the other person. In other words, how can you make it special for them?

Two: You can include friends in the ideas and details, but they cannot go with you—whether it is a dinner or a trip abroad.

Here are a few examples of our best ideas to inspire you.

Joe, who is naturally romantic, had the honor of starting the new rules on our ninth anniversary. For nine days leading up to the date, he gave me nine of something every day: nine roses, nine cards, nine chocolates, even nine soft kisses.

In return, I made it clear we had just made a great discovery and the change was made permanent.

I was not to be outdone on our 10th anniversary.

So, with help from a friend, I created a scavenger hunt with clues taking Joe through the homes of 10 of our friends. The caveat was that Joe loves to talk and he loves our friends, so the friends also enforced a time limit. On the 10th and last clue, I was waiting for him at a hotel to make all his anniversary dreams come true.

Our surprises have varied widely over the years, from an exotic vacation for our 25th, to funny nights at home when we had no money.

It has made our anniversaries special, as each of us secretly plans something that will be meaningful to the other. (You can also use this idea as a guideline for setting up rules for family vacations, holidays, or other events so they don't just become another boring milestone or obligation.)

What fun things would you love to do for your partner?

82 I Love...

83 I Love...

84 I Love...

Add the fun and wild things you love doing with your partner. Include your indulgences, wickedness, signature moves, wild dreams, favorite body parts and all their qualities you shouldn't brag about—but love to anyway.

85 I Love...

86 I Love...

87 I Love...

88 I Love...

89 I Love...

90 I Love...

16

It's Up to You...

I love Joe and I've always loved him.

Love is a lot of things, but it's mostly a decision. That tingle and lust you feel the first months or years you know a person is actually not love. Those are feelings. And feelings are not facts.

Love is what you see in the rearview mirror of your life. Love is what you do when you really don't want to do something, and yet you do it because it makes the person you are committed to happy.

Let's face it, it's a whole different world out there than just a few years ago. We live in a time where we are told to focus on ourselves and our needs. And, true, we all need to take care of ourselves. But has this self-obsession really made us any happier? When I meet a truly happy person, the topic they talk about the most is the joy they feel when they serve others.

I've lost a child, I've had health challenges, and, probably like many of you, I've gone through most of the challenges that can destroy a relationship. But I'm happy and I love my husband.

If you've ever really loved your partner, but don't feel that love now, and you want it to work, but you believe that you'd be happier if only they'd change just a little bit of this or that? Experience has shown me that kind of "yes, but..." thinking won't work.

Now, my advice comes with a caveat that you may not like.

If your relationship isn't working, and, with all your heart, you really want it to, there is really just one thing you can do: change yourself. The responsibility is on you.

Relationships fail at a far higher rate than they succeed. If we continue to look for solutions outside ourselves, the sadness, affairs, broken homes, hurt children, and the number of divorces, will all continue to increase.

It's possible that everything you want, and need, is still right there for you. You may have realized that Joe didn't change a lot, but I did. I stopped looking at what I wasn't getting and I began to look closely at what I wasn't doing. It's complicated. But here's one true thing: the day I decided that I would change was one of the greatest days of my life.

I realized I was the only person I could control. I decided that Joe and I were worth the effort and my relationship was what I wanted. The day I decided I would change, led me to the relationship that I'd always wanted.

By and large, most happiness is a decision. While the reasons Joe and I survived have to do with timing, luck,